# ᶻC HORSES
# GOLDIE
# THE WISE!

Diane W. Keaster

illustrated by Debbie Page

1

ISBN 0-9721496-6-X
ISBN 978-0972149662

# Printed in U.S.A

# ZC HORSES
# GOLDIE
# THE WISE!

To my brother Bruce who let me ride with him and gave me the idea about getting Chick.

# ZC HORSES
## SERIES

Be part of them all!

Chick - The Beginning!

Chick - The Saddle Horse!

Chick - The Mom!

Luke - The First!

Barbie - The Best!

Leroy - The Stallion!

*And Many More!*

# ᶻC HORSES
# GOLDIE
# THE WISE!

# *1*
# THE BEGINNING

Being a rancher runs in families. If you grow up on a ranch, it is probably because your mother or father grew up on one. Their mother or father probably grew up on one. That is how it was for me. I grew up on a ranch. My father's father was a rancher. Both of my father's grandfathers were ranchers. My father's grandfathers were Edward Keaster and Robert

Murphy. These were my great-grandfathers.

Edward Keaster fought in the Civil War before he became a rancher. He sought adventure after the army. As did Lewis and Clark, my great-grandfather went up the gigantic Missouri River. This was in the mid-1800's. He arrived at Fort Benton, Montana. Fort Benton was the last spot on the Missouri a house-like steamboat could travel. There were large, roaring waterfalls past this point. These are the falls Lewis and Clark dubbed the 'Great Falls' on their trek.

Grandpa Keaster worked hard to start a living when he arrived in Montana. One thing he did was hunt massive buffalo and wildlife. This was to provide food for soldiers. They were at a fort called Fort Shaw.

When Grandpa Keaster had enough money, he bought teams of oxen. Oxen are the male members of the cattle family. They are used for draft. A draft animal pulls a wagon. Grandpa Keaster then became a bull-whacker. A bull-whacker is the person that walks beside the ox. He kept the ox moving in the right direction. This was sometimes difficult since they did not want to go all of the time.

Grandpa Keaster hauled wood and other goods into Canada. This meant walking hundreds and hundreds of miles beside the hard-working beasts of burden. He encountered raging thunderstorms and biting blizzards. He also had to worry about thieves attacking him along the dusty, rough routes. He had to have thick soles on his boots!

Grandpa Keaster always desired to be a rancher. Once he had enough money, he went to Deer Lodge, Montana. There he purchased a herd of cows. A grueling 200-mile cattle drive then began. The cows traveled over high, snowy mountain peaks. They moved slowly in front of his horse. Their heads hung to the ground. They were too tired to run away.

Toward the end of the drive, the cows had to swim across the great Missouri River. It was very wide. The cows had to keep forging the cold, strong current once they jumped in. Once across, they found their new home on Grandpa Keaster's ranch in the Highwood Mountains. The beautiful

Highwood Mountains can be seen by many towns including Belt, Highwood, Fort Benton and Great Falls. It was above these mountains where I often watched the amazing Northern Lights. They darted their show of colors through the silent night sky.

Grandpa Keaster was one of the earliest ranchers in the area. He was thought to be a good cattle and horseman. His sons, including my grandfather, were considered to be the top horsemen around. My father, in turn, followed in his father's tracks. He had a wonderful bond with horses. His children and grandchildren followed in his footsteps.

Working with cows is a skill that is born into you. Another skill that comes naturally is working with and loving horses. That is a skill I was meant to have. It was passed down from generation to generation.

The one thing I loved about the horses was seeing the different generations. Watching Chick provide me with her babies was a joy. Then to see her grandchildren was even more wonderful.

One daughter of Chick's was a true joy. She was very wise and fun to work with. She had adventures as did my Great-grandpa Keaster.

# 2

# BABY THREE

Chick had been a fantastic mare, or mother horse, for me. I enjoyed raising her babies. The best baby so far was Barbie. I was glad I had bought Barbie's father Dan. He and Chick gave me the gray mare I had always wanted.

Barbie was now a spry one year old. She was what is called a yearling. She had been weaned for several months. Being weaned means she did not need to drink milk from her mother anymore. A foal, or baby horse, is usually weaned when it is about four to six months old. When a foal is weaned, it is taken away from its mother for awhile. Later they are put back together. The foal does not nurse, or drink milk from its mom anymore. The maturing foal can survive on its own at that time. Even though Barbie was weaned, she and Chick still showed love for each other. You could tell they were mother and daughter.

Since Barbie was so special, I looked forward to having her baby sister or brother. I knew Chick and Dan would give me another wonderful baby. This would be Chick's third baby.

Again I had to wait the long eleven months before Chick had her baby. Since Barbie was gray, I wondered what color this baby would be. Its velvety attire may be black since Chick's mother was black. The foal could be sorrel, or red, since Chick's father was sorrel. Dan was gray so the foal might be gray like its sister Barbie. It did not matter how much I guessed. I had to wait to see!

Chick was pastured right next to the house when she was going to foal. She was always in sight. Every day her tummy grew bigger and bigger. It was like watching a balloon being slowly blown up. I knew she would not pop, though! I felt the baby kick when I set my head against her soft belly. This was what I did before Barbie was born.

Since it was the spring of the year, the trees were just showing their leaves. The breeze made the green hands shiver against the sky. The grass was like a plush carpet under Chick. Her golden body looked beautiful against the green sea. A rainbow of flowers was starting to bloom. I always liked to pick yellow buttercups when I strolled through the pasture. The purple rooster head was my favorite.

Chick stayed in the bottom of the coulee, or small valley. It was too hard for her to carry her extra load up the hill. A spring half way up the hill provided a small stream of water for Chick to drink from. The stream looked like a silver snake slithering down the steep hillside. A spring is an area where water comes right out of the dry ground.

Shazzy, my small dog, watched Chick all through the day. So did I. I had never yet seen a foal drop, or be born.

On April 24, I knew the baby would soon be born. I checked on Chick all through the night. It was hard to see because the moon was hiding behind the star-filled, black sky. The stars winked at me. It was as though they were laughing, "She'll never get to see this baby born!" Nothing happened all night.

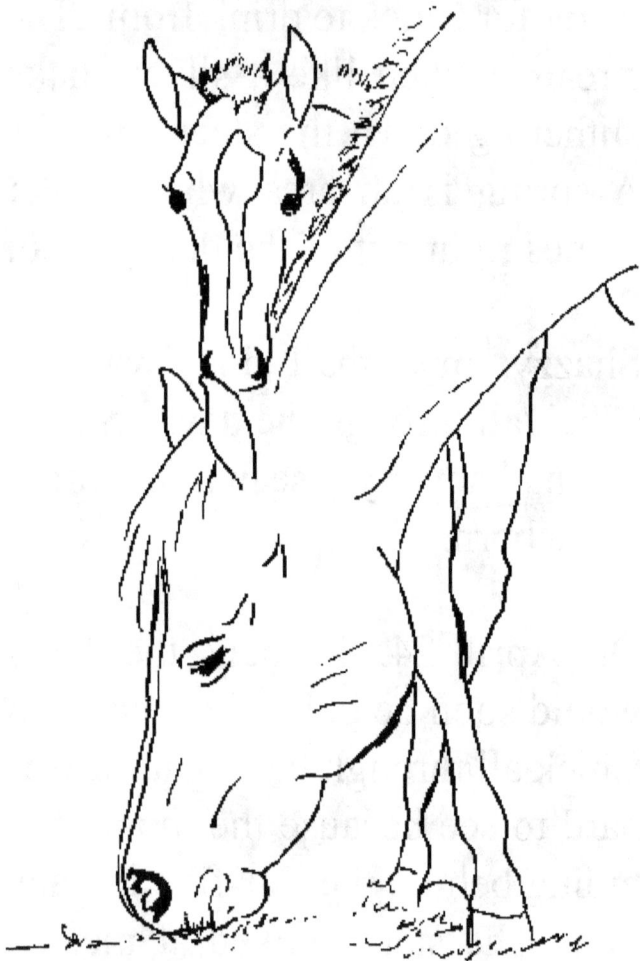

The next morning was April 25. It was the date both Chick and Barbie were born. I had been up all through the chilly night. The sun was just peeking from behind the climbing hill. Flitting robins sang their early morning song.

I slowly plodded out to look at Chick. I figured there was no sense rushing since nothing happened the few hours earlier when I was out. What a shock! There it was. At Chick's feet lay a beautiful, palomino filly, or girl. Although Chick was a deep golden palomino, her new foal was a lighter palomino. There was no doubt that it was Chick's baby. It had the same exact blaze, or white down its face. Since this foal looked so much like her mom, I dubbed her Goldie.

Once again, Chick was the perfect mother. She smothered Goldie with love. I heard her continually tossing a loving whinny her way.

Right away, so Goldie would like people, I held her in my arms. Unlike Barbie, Goldie did not put up a fight at all. She stood quietly while I slid my hands over her soft coat. Her dark brown eyes had such a gentle look to them. Her silky white eyelashes curled to the sky. Her pure white mane and tail felt like silk.

When I felt the muscles in her body tense, I whispered in her ear, "I won't hurt you, Goldie." Her body relaxed. Chick's reassuring nicker helped calm her down, too.

Since Goldie and Barbie had the same mother and father, they were called full sisters. This meant, too, they would be a lot alike. Even though I could tell right away that Goldie was very smart, I was concerned about halter breaking her. I remembered how Barbie was!

I was in for a shock when the training began!

# 3

# THE TEACHER

A halter is a nylon, leather or rope piece that goes over the horse's nose and head. This is placed on the horse's head so you can lead them, hold them or tie them up. A newborn foal has never been handled. At times they will fight the first time they wear a halter.

Barbie despised wearing her first halter. She fought me terribly. She pulled back with all her strength. She snorted and tromped her feet. I was holding onto the end of the lead rope. The lead rope is attached to the halter under the horse's chin.

Goldie was to wear the same tiny blue halter Barbie wore. I had my arms around Goldie's small frame. I felt I was holding a plush teddy bear. I held the halter in my right hand. With my hand by Goldie's right cheek, I pulled the halter over her nose. I heard her every exhale. Slowly I fastened the halter behind Goldie's ears. It looked so pretty on Goldie's soft, yellow face.

With the halter fastened and the lead rope connected, I was ready for the fight. I let go of Goldie's body. I was ready for her to fly away from me as Barbie did. Goldie stood and studied me with her kind, wise eyes. I walked away to lead her. She followed like an eager puppy. The shuffling of her pint-size hooves, or feet, sounded in unison with mine. It was as if she already knew what to do.

Goldie was fun to handle. She was very smart and easy to get along with. When she was a few months old, she and Chick were pastured along the Missouri River. This is the gigantic river Lewis and Clark followed. Goldie could have watched them go by if she had been born then! To train Goldie, I sometimes led her along the river through the aspen trees. Chick always walked beside her. We enjoyed listening to the soothing hum of the river flowing by. The aspen trees waved to us with their small green flags. Robins hopped from tree to tree, singing their song to us as we strolled. I could have stayed there forever!

Goldie taught her mom a lesson near this pasture. I needed to load both Goldie and Chick into a two-horse trailer. This type of trailer is not very wide. Since Chick was such a large horse, she did not like to load. Goldie jumped right in her side of the trailer. Chick fought me. She did not want to get in. Then Goldie whinnied at her mom. It was as though she was telling her to jump in beside her.

With a leap, jump is what Chick did. I thought she was going to go right through the front of her tiny transportation. I am sure it seemed big to Goldie. To Chick, it was probably like sitting in a soup can!

Goldie always acted wisely. I could always trust her. She was willing to do anything I asked of her.

Things might be different riding her, though!

# 4

# SO WISE

Goldie's accepting the halter made me excited to ride her. I felt if she was that wise and gentle, she would not mind me breaking her, or training her to be ridden.

When Goldie turned two years old, it was time she was broke. It was the spring of the year. Just like when she was born, the trees started bearing their leaves. Grass was turning its luscious green. Baby calves dotted the pastures. New foals pranced around their moms.

The first time I rode Goldie was at the house. I remembered the second day I rode her mom. It was in the same wooden corral. I remembered seeing my father framed by the big picture window in the house. He was waving to me with a grin from ear to ear. Chick had just bucked me off. I did not think it was very funny.

I was hoping the same thing would not happen with Goldie. I was nervous when I put my foot into the round stirrup. Goldie glanced back at me. She wondered what I was doing. Her body tensed. All the gleeful birds became silenced.

I pushed myself up and eased into the cold hard saddle. I was ready for her to blow.

Just like with halter breaking, Goldie acted like I had always ridden her. She walked off like a broke horse.

The second day of riding arrived. We had to move cows to a different pasture. I took my chances using Goldie to gather. When riding a horse the first few times, a pen keeps them contained. A horse has more room to run and buck in an open pasture. There are more things to spook them. Rabbits might hop out. Rattle snakes may strike.

I got on Goldie in a pen first. Then I opened the gate. Belt Butte gazed at us from across the valley. This pasture at the Old Place was surrounded by the Highwood, Big Belt and Little Belt Mountain Ranges. The Rocky Mountain Front was in the far distance. It was along this fence line that Barbie kept taking the fencing pliers out of my father's pants pocket. She grabbed them gently with her teeth. Away she then flung them. She was just a foal then. In my father's eyes, she was a nuisance.

Goldie looked out the gate. Her furry ears were straight up. She sighed.... then stepped right out. Immediately she watched the cows. When close to one, her ears were pinned back. Her mother and father were both cowy, or liked to work cows. She was, too.

The cows and riders took off loping across the field. Sometimes when breaking a horse, the horse wants to buck when you first lope on it. Goldie started loping along with everyone else. Her mane and tail flowed in the air. She was very smooth and eager to keep up with the cows. Bucking did not cross her mind.

Nothing at all bothered Goldie. She was not spooked about anything. Not even a scurrying gopher scared her. She did everything I asked of her.

Since Goldie was green, or not broke, I had to gently pull her nose in the direction I wanted her to head. I only had to bring her nose around a few times. Then she knew when the reign touched the opposite side of her neck she was to turn. That way I did not have to pull her nose anymore. She neck reigned.

A reign is a strap of leather attached to the bit. The bit is in the horse's mouth to control them. The other end of the reign is in the rider's hand.

The end of this second-day riding was much different from when riding Chick. Goldie had already been on her first cattle drive. I remember my father saying, "It's just like in the movies." In the old-time westerns, the cowboy jumped on a horse for the first time and loped off after the cattle. That is pretty much what Goldie did.

Goldie was very wise about learning so far. She was eager to do everything I asked of her.

One of the scariest things for a horse to learn was now to come!

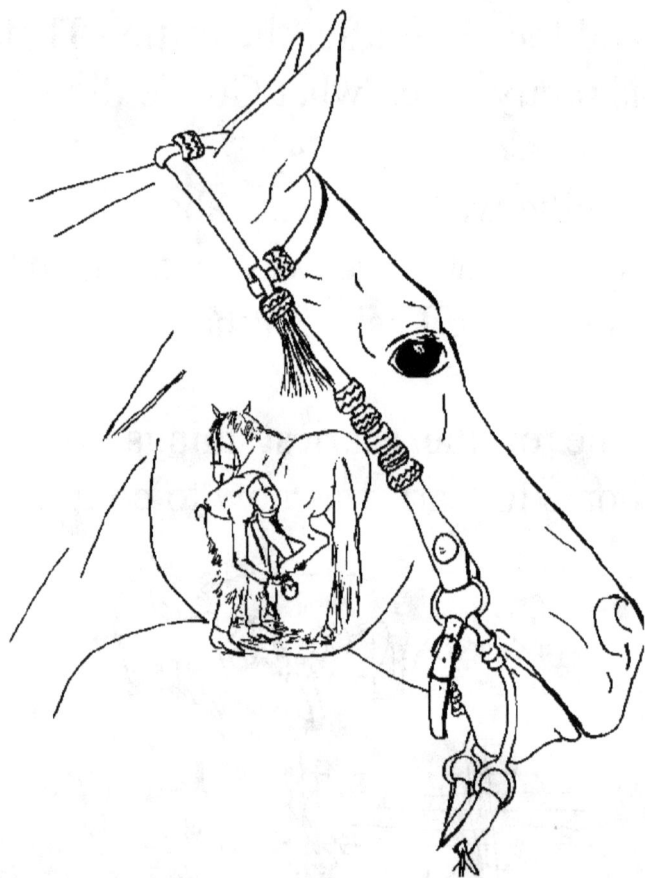

# 5

# NEW SHOES

When a horse is ridden often, they need protection on their hooves. A horse's hoof is like your finger nail. It grows. If the hoof gets too long, like a fingernail, it may chip off and hurt the horse. Also, if the hoof is grown out too long, a horse is forced to stand on the back of its hoof. Standing on the back of the hoof can cause the horse to become lame, or crippled. If a horse is in a rocky pasture, its hooves will stay worn down. If the hooves grow out, they need to be trimmed. This quite often needs to be done every six to eight weeks.

The hoof is a natural protection for the foot. If the horse is ridden too much without additional protection, its hoof will become worn down too much. Then its foot will become tender. There is no protection.

Iron plates are put on horses hooves to protect them. These are called horse shoes. A farrier is a person that puts shoes on horses, or shoes them. When a horse has shoes put on, it is said they are shod (rhymes with cod). The farrier also trims hooves.

Sometimes it is very difficult to shoe a horse the first time. The horse has no idea what is going on. They sometimes will fight, kick, strike, or pull back.

Since I was riding Goldie quite a bit she needed to be shod. I was concerned about how she would act toward the farrier. I held her head so she would be still.

The farrier picked up her front hoof. Goldie wobbled on three legs. The farrier trimmed off any extra hoof with nippers. She threw her worried look at me when she heard the sharp "Snip, snip, snip." Nippers are strong, sharp pliers with very long handles.

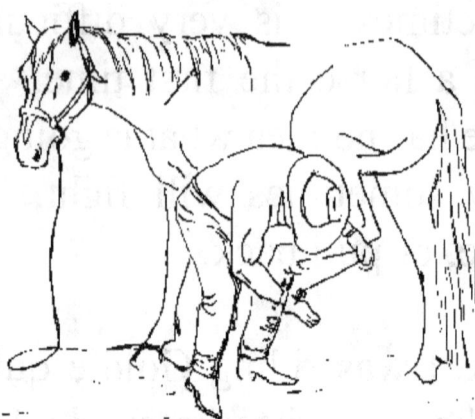

With a file, he smoothed the outer edge of the hoof. Goldie looked back at him out of the corner of her eye. Her soft ears turned toward him, also.

The farrier intently studied the shape of the hoof. He gently set the hoof down. He needed to know what shape to make the shoe. Goldie was happy to be able to stand on all four feet and relax. She thought we were finished!

The farrier then grabbed out of his truck a shoe he felt would fit Goldie. She was young still so had small feet. One of the smallest sizes of shoes is a double '0'. That is two zeros or a double ott (rhymes with bought). The next size is an ott, or just one zero. As the shoes get larger, they are sized from one to two and on up. Goldie wore an ott.

The farrier placed the shoe on his anvil. An anvil is made out of iron and extremely heavy. Goldie watched intently the whole time. With a hammer, the shoe was shaped like Goldie's hoof. She wondered what the loud "Cling, clang, cling" of the hammer was all about. Then, with small nails in his mouth and the shoe in his hand, the farrier picked up Goldie's hoof. Once again Goldie was standing on three legs.

The farrier had Goldie's leg bent and pressed between his legs. He placed the shoe on her hoof. The sharp nails were gently tapped through a hole in the shoe into the edge of Goldie's hoof. Like our finger nails, there is no feeling there. This did not hurt her. Even though Goldie questioned what the farrier was doing, she never fought him. Goldie had to be patient. If not, she could be quicked. This is when a nail goes into the sensitive flesh underneath the hooves. It is painful if something goes under our fingernails. This is very painful for the horse, too.

The six or eight nails were in place. Their sharp points poked through the outer side of Goldie's hoof. They were snipped off with the nippers. The ends of the nails were then bent over. This was so the rough edges did not cut either Goldie or the farrier. Goldie's leg was pulled ahead and put on a stand to do this. The ends were then filed smooth to make them safer.

There was a little hoof sticking out beyond the edge of the shoe, so this was then filed off. Now Goldie had a perfectly shaped and protected hoof. The other three hooves were shod in the same way. A horse will usually get better about being shod each time it is done. Goldie was good from the start!

She was even great about things most horses never do!

# 6

# THE TRIP

When a horse is young, it is not accustomed to everything. It takes riding in different situations to feel comfortable. When Goldie was two, she went for a trip.

In the Fall, we went into the mountains to look for elk. An elk is of the deer family. It is much larger than a deer. Its antlers are gigantic.

We were going to ride behind Holter Lake near Helena. This is the capital of Montana. This area was called the Beartooth Game Range. Goldie was very young and did not know much yet. I was taking her along to get used to things. Barbie was the horse I would ride. She had already taken the trip. She loved these times. Since Goldie had not been there, she might get frightened about the new sights.

This ride can be a scary time for a young horse. It starts before the sun comes up. The brisk air sends chills through you. Darkness surrounds you. The frightening howls of coyotes echo through your ears.

Goldie was nervous being in the horse trailer with so many other horses. She had never been with so many. She could have gotten hurt.

Goldie was planning on my riding her. She did not know I was leaving her tied to the hitching post at camp. A hitching post is a horizontal post connected to two sturdy, standing posts. The standing posts are several feet apart. The horse is tied to the horizontal post.

We rode to where we set up camp. It was a beautiful ride through fresh-smelling pine trees. A clear rippling creek (rhymes with stick in Montana) sang to us as we climbed the mountain. I rode

Barbie and led Goldie. Goldie packed some of the food and clothes to be used during the trip.

Once we arrived at the camp site, I unsaddled Goldie and Barbie. They were able to rest at the hitching post. Goldie needed this rest. It was a long, hard ride for her.

The hitching post was right next to the wall tent. A wall tent is made out of thick canvas. It is held up by small trees or by a rope tied to trees around it. The tent has tall walls so you are able to walk around in it. Goldie and Barbie enjoyed being able to watch everything I was doing.

Once camp was all set up and a fire was going, I decided to ride Goldie. Her eyes softened as I walked to her. She was happy to see me. She was happy to be ridden. Barbie whinnied gently. I did not put a bridle on Goldie. I swung the lead rope around her neck and tied it. This acted as the reins.

Without a saddle, I jumped on Goldie. I did not know what to expect. She had not yet been ridden bareback. This is when you ride without a saddle. Goldie did not mind me at all on her bare back.

Off we went enjoying the beauty creation provides. The smell of the camp fire followed us. Mountain peaks rose above us. Eagles soared high in their fresh pool of air. Their, "Screech, Screech," fell to us.

We rode to the sparkling creek we enjoyed on the way in. I figured Goldie would be thirsty. When a young horse is just learning, they are usually afraid to cross water.

Rather than get a drink, Goldie stepped right into the creek. With the water past her ankles, she walked across. Just like her sister, she loved the water.

When we got back to camp, I tied Goldie up by Barbie. A gelding was on the other side of Barbie. I gave them their supper and told them goodnight. They did not want me to leave. I let Barbie know I would be riding her the next day. I needed to get my sleep and had to leave them.

From the tent, silence covered me. My sleeping bag kept out the crisp air. I then heard the cold water of the stream slicing through the darkness. The howls of coyotes and hoots of owls provided harmony to the creek's melodious song. Deep into the night I woke up to the sounds of the horses shuffling around and squealing. They soon settled down. I was not concerned.

Preparation began long before the sun rose. I slid into the darkness to saddle up Barbie. As I neared her, my heart dropped. Barbie was holding one leg up. The commotion during the night was the gelding kicking her. There was no way she could make the trip. I was forced to ride Goldie.

Even though Goldie questioned riding in the dark, she did well. The majestic elk dashed close to us. Goldie was not afraid. She enjoyed the beautiful day. Once again, she did everything I asked of her.

Goldie not only proved to be wise but she was something else!

# 7

# SO GENTLE

Using Goldie in the mountains showed one more time how wise she was. Because of this, she was very gentle. She knew riding in different areas would not hurt her.

My three nieces were looking at Goldie soon after I started riding her. I asked them if they wanted to sit on her. They said yes. I put Rachel on Goldie's back. Goldie turned her sweet brown eyes toward me, but she stood still.

Sarah wanted on. I slid her behind Rachel. Sarah wrapped her arms tightly around Rachel. The girls giggled. Goldie once again looked back. Then it was Laura's turn. I smoothly slipped her over Goldie's back. Right away Laura grabbed Sarah.

Goldie gave the three giggling girls a ride. It did not bother her a bit that they were there. If Goldie

had not been so gentle, I would not
have put the girls on her back.
Most young, green (or inexperi-
enced) horses scare easily. They
jump or buck if they are scared. I
was sure Goldie would not do such
a thing.

Whenever I rode Goldie across the
countryside, nothing scared her. It
did not matter if she heard the omi-
nous rattle of the rattle snake. A
coyote streaking across the horizon was of no concern. A ground-
hog sticking his head out of the
rocks caused no panic. A ground-
hog is also called a woodchuck. It
is a small, furry animal with large
front teeth. It digs tunnels into the
ground. Pheasants rocketing from
the ground did not startle Goldie

either. They hid in the tall grass until you were right on them.

Goldie trusted everyone. She was always willing to be caught. Some horses are very bad about that. They will run from you when you want to catch them. When Goldie heard the honk of the truck's horn, she came running. Snow or dust kicked up behind her. Sending my shrill whistle through the clear air caused her to break into a high lope. Goldie always loved the attention. She always wanted to talk to me.

Goldie was not afraid of anything. Because of this, she trusted everyone and everything. She did not think anything would hurt her.

She was wrong, though!

# 8

# SPION KOP

We had another ranch far from home. It was called Spion Kop. This was an area of rolling hills set against the Highwood Mountains. It was between two small Montana towns called Raynesford and Geyser.

The grass at the Spion Kop ranch was very plentiful. This was where Luke ended up having four black legs. It was also where I rode Chick into the bog chasing the bull.

We pastured cows in this windy pasture into the winter. When the snow got too deep for the cows to eat, we moved them home. This was usually a tough cattle drive. Many times a blinding blizzard hit. We could not stop, though, because we had to get the cows out of the snow. Drifts built barriers so that we could not move.

Goldie had the opportunity to go on this cattle drive. We first gathered the cows together. Then we moved them across several large pastures. The frosty Fall air had turned the green grass to brown. The aroma of winter teased the sleeping stalks of feed.

Goldie loved gliding up and down the roller coaster hills. A rolling sea of red, black and white moved before her. The sound of sticks breaking, dirt pushing and hard hooves hitting rocks rang though the blue sky.

At the edge of the last pasture, we pushed the herd through a gate onto a narrow, black highway. This was a very busy highway. It ran between Great Falls and Billings, the two largest cities in Montana. We had to travel about twenty miles along this trek.

There were several bridges we had to cross. This was the only way we could get across the winding

Otter Creek. Goldie was apprehensive about her first bridge. The hollow sound of her every step echoing under the bridge worried her.

The cows stretched out nicely in between the bridges. The rhythmic "Clunk, clunk" of their hooves on the asphalt almost put me to sleep. When we got to a bridge, though, they bunched up. They were afraid to cross. Many turned

around to head in the opposite direction. We pushed forcefully against the frantic cows. Goldie did not know what to think about the hollering and shoving. With much effort, the cows finally sifted through the concrete monsters.

This cattle drive took a full day. It began before the sun came up and ended at dark. Goldie's first time on this drive exhausted her. She was ready for a break at home.

Goldie spent her winters at Spion Kop. There was plenty of grass for her all winter long. The howling wind blew many areas of dinner open for her. I visited her through the frigid season.

One arctic day  I went to see Goldie.  I saw from a distance something was wrong.  Her head was hanging.  Her legs were spread out.  I could not imagine what had happened.  I rushed to her.

On Goldie's back were several deep scratches.  Streaks of red marked her pale yellow color.  Her thick winter coat was matted down by the wounds.

It was obvious.  A cougar had attacked Goldie.  A cougar is also called a mountain lion.  It is a gigantic, vicious cat.  The quick-footed bully had jumped on her.  It planted all four clawed paws, gouging Goldie's rounded back.

I comforted Goldie. She needed it. She must have put up a good fight. A cougar can kill animals bigger than Goldie, like elk. The wounds were not as bad as they could have been. They healed quickly. Goldie did not trust the cougar for very long!

Goldie not only took care of herself after the attack but others!

# 9

# THE MOM

Just like with Chick and Barbie, it was time for Goldie to become a mother. As wise, loving and kind as Goldie was, I knew she would make a great mom. She would take good care of a baby.

Through the years, Goldie had several babies. One was very special though.

I wanted to have a paint foal. A paint is quarter horse bred but has white sections over its body. I wanted Goldie to have the first paint baby I raised.

Goldie was a quarter horse. This meant I needed to find a paint stallion. At least one of the parents has to be paint to have a paint foal.

I knew of a wonderful buckskin paint stallion. A buckskin horse has a golden-colored body. Its mane and tail are black. The bottoms of its legs are black, too. A buckskin paint, then, has white sections throughout its body.

This stallion's name was Royal Touch O Gold. He had been used as a rope horse, like Barbie. He was also used as a cutting horse, like Goldie's father. He stood close to sixteen hands. A hand is four inches.

With Goldie as this baby's mother and Royal as its father, it should be very athletic and cowy. It also should be beautiful!

Once again, the eleven months seemed to go on forever. It was fun watching Goldie grow larger every day. Many questions went through my head. Would the baby have any white on it? Sometimes even if the mother or father is a paint, there is no extra white on the baby. Would it be a filly (girl) or colt (boy)? What color would its body be? Both Goldie's and Royal's bodies were yellow.

Goldie's grandmother (Chick's mom) was black, though. I had to wait and see what color the baby was!

Finally the time drew near. Goldie was in a grassy pasture on top of the coulee. She could see in the distance the four mountain ranges that decorate the horizon. On April 18, all of my questions were answered. The baby was finally here!

It was a bright sunny day. Spring was waking up its bountiful floral arrangement. One sniff filled my senses with fresh grass and wild flowers. Little dots of blue, yellow, pink and red were popping through the green covering. Trees were again clothing themselves.

Goldie gave birth to her best foal. It was a filly. She was first called Whiskers. This was because of her never-ending hairs on her tiny nose. My brother Gary still calls her Whiskers. The foal's final name was Golden Lovely Lily.

Lily's coat was grullo. The grullo color is such a dark golden that it looks almost brown. The bottom half of her mane was white. So was the top part of her tail. She had four white stockings (a stocking is white high up on the leg). There also were white sections throughout her body. Goldie certainly had her paint!

Lily was just as friendly and wise as her mom. When we went to hold her, she peeked around Goldie. I think she thought we might not see her!

I knew Lily would grow up to be a wonderful mare. Why wouldn't she be with Goldie as her mother! Her best friends were Classy and Belle.

Goldie was a good mother to all her babies. She was even more so with Lily. I wondered if Goldie remembered how good Chick was to her when she was a baby.

The motherly instinct never ends!

# *10*

# FAMILY LOVE

Chick gave me many happy memories. So did Goldie. I always enjoyed working with her and riding her.

Something that always amazes me, even to this day, is the closeness there is between Chick, Barbie and Goldie. There is no doubt they are mother and daughters. It does not matter if they are apart for periods of time. They always have that special whinny for each other.

They always greet each other. You can see the love they have for each other.

Just like we are close with our mother and brothers or sisters, horses do the same. No matter what changes come in their lives they are still family. They always have that special love for one another.

Goldie will always be the horse I remember as wise. She never did anything wrong. She was always kind, loving and gentle. I will always thank her and love her for that.

Goldie's time of having babies is not over. The father of her next baby is a beautiful buckskin quarter horse. How fun it will be to see it and enjoy another of Goldie's babies and Chick's grandchild!

# ᶻC HORSES SERIES

Now that you have learned Goldie's story, meet Chick's fourth baby, Chickadee! Get to know her odd, special mother! See how special she is! Go into the mountains with her! See how different she is from her sisters Barbie and Goldie! Learn what her special quality is! You will adore Chickadee after reading the eighth book in the **'ZC HORSES'** series, *"CHICKADEE-THE TRAVELER!"*. Be sure to be there to greet her!!

ᶻC HORSES SERIES #8

## Chickadee-TheTraveler!
### by Diane W. Keaster
### Coming June 2004

To My Reader:

I was born and raised on a ranch near a little town called Belt, Montana. After receiving my B.S. in Business Education from Montana State University, I taught high school business. I then moved on to other facets of employment.

The whole time, I was team roping and raising, breaking and training horses. The profession I fell into by mistake was trading horses. Throughout my life, I have handled hundreds of horses, all which have a story of their own.

My sons, Cole and Augustus, loved reading stories about horses when they were small and I loved reading the stories to them. That is why I am writing these books. I want to tell the stories of the creatures I love to the children I love.

My husband Chuck, sons Cole and Augustus and myself all live in beautiful Salmon, Idaho with Page, Cowboy, Maggie, Chance (Strange), Shedaisey (dogs), Onyx, Weasel, Skunk (cats), George (parrot), Barbie, Classy, Belle, Lily, Annie, Goldie, Cash (horses), Lucy (goose), and many chickens and rabbits.

I thank Jehovah our Creator for giving us such a wonderful, beautiful animal to love and write about!

Enjoy the stories!

# Order Form
## ZC HORSES SERIES

Don't miss out on any part of the lives of Chick and her many babies and friends! Experience all of the rides, joys and sorrows. Don't be left out!

| | |
|---|---|
| ___ Chick-The Beginning! (Spring 2001) | $7.95 |
| ___ Chick-The Saddle Horse! (September 2001) | $7.95 |
| ___ Chick-The Mom! (April 2002) | $7.95 |
| ___ Luke-The First! (September 2002) | $7.95 |
| ___ Barbie-The Best! (Oct. 2002) | $7.95 |
| ___ Leroy-The Stallion! (September 2003) | $7.95 |
| ___ Goldie-The Wise! (March 2004) | $7.95 |
| ___ Chickadee-The Traveler! (June 2004) | $7.95 |
| ___ Darby-The Cow Dog! (September 2004) | $7.95 |
| ___ Sonny-The Spectacular! (November 2004) | $7.95 |

### UPCOMING TITLES

| | |
|---|---|
| Tawny-The Beauty! | Apple-The Joy! |
| Onie-The Roanie! | Belle-The Sweetie! |
| Classy-The Special! | Lily-The Pretty Paint! |
| Black Jack-The Great ! | Slick-TheFriend! |

Also read about Cider, Buck, Nellie, Junie, Eagle, Smokey, Sarge, Tex, Radar and many more!

-------------------------------------------------------------------------

**ZC HORSES SERIES, 8 Hknsn Ln., Salmon, ID 83467**
**(208) 756-7947**
**www.zchorses.com**
**Email: zchorses@hotmail.com**

Please send me the books I have checked above. I am enclosing US $____(please add $2/bk to cover shipping and handling). Send check or money order, please.

NAME_____

ADDRESS_____

CITY/STATE/ZIP_____

PHONE_____

# NOTES AND PICTURES!!!!

# NOTES AND PICTURES!!!!

# NOTES AND PICTURES!!!!

# NOTES AND PICTURES!!!!

# NOTES AND PICTURES!!!!

# NOTES AND PICTURES!!!!

# NOTES AND PICTURES!!!!

# NOTES AND PICTURES!!!!

www.ingramcontent.com/pod-product-compliance
Lightning Source LLC
Chambersburg PA
CBHW050544280326
41933CB00011B/1715